Ask Mi-Ling!

To: Diana
Live your dreams
Today!

Mi-Ling "2006"

Ask Mi-Ling!

✦

When you want the truth about decorating

Written by Mi-Ling Stone Poole
Edited by Lisa Shearer & Richard Mize
Cover design by Victor Driver

iUniverse, Inc.
New York Lincoln Shanghai

Ask Mi-Ling!
When you want the truth about decorating

iUniverse books may be ordered through booksellers or by contacting:

iUniverse
2021 Pine Lake Road, Suite 100
Lincoln, NE 68512
www.iuniverse.com
1-800-Authors (1-800-288-4677)

Front Cover: The top right photograph shows the interior entryway of Mi-Ling's home. The lower right photograph shows her dining room. Both spaces were decorated by Mi-Ling Stone Poole.

ISBN-13: 978-0-595-38310-8 (pbk)
ISBN-13: 978-0-595-82681-0 (ebk)
ISBN-10: 0-595-38310-6 (pbk)
ISBN-10: 0-595-82681-4 (ebk)

Printed in the United States of America

Dedication

To my husband Edward—you are my rock and the love of my life

To my children—Tiffany and Eddie find your passion

To my brother Tony—you inspired me

To my family and friends—Thank you for your support

"Life begins when you find your passion"

— Mi-Ling Stone Poole

Contents

Acknowledgements

To my husband Edward and my children, Tiffany and Eddie, thanks for putting up with all of my madness and still supporting me. To my parents, Rosa Lee Handley and Anthony M. Stone, thanks for believing in me. To Norman Handley, thanks for all of your guidance. To my sisters, Kim Lee Stone and Tonia M. Stone, thanks for listening to my columns over the phone. To Larry Turner, thanks for your construction advice. To Carole and Vernon Small, and Katie and Louis Ervin, you have always been there for me. To the late Frank C. Kent, you lit the fire. To Genita Walker, thanks for all of your love and encouragement. To Sandy Martin, you inspired me! To Victor Driver, your artwork is amazing. A special thanks to my friends at the Edmond Women's Club for allowing me to invade their privacy and write about their beautiful homes.

To John and Courtney Gray, thanks for your support and encouragement. To Jeri and Dixie Harris, you're my biggest fans! To Sam, Mitra and my other son Matt, thanks for believing. To Denise and Marion Jordon, thanks for giving me my first professional writing assignment at the *Kansas City Globe*.

To my dear friends Joe and Diana Carter, thank you for allowing me to feature your gorgeous home. To Rick and Carol Goff, your drive is inspiring. To Rhealene and Danny Cook, you were my first feature story and I'll never forget all of your help. To Joey, Heather, Ryan and Nugget from Wild 97.9, you guys opened the door for me in Oklahoma City, and I'll always love ya! To Jack and Ron from Kiss 98.9 what can I say, you are the bad boys of radio. We took decorating to another level!

To Thelma and Kenneth Poole, thanks for your support. To Milton McCourtie, thanks for listening and all of your advice. To Janet Lowrey, thanks for being my sounding board. To Mike Cooper and Stanley Smith, I couldn't have done it without you guys. To Shelby and Julian, follow your dreams. To my cousins, carry on the dream. To my friends at the *Edmond Sun*: Lisa Shearer, you believed in my vision and I couldn't have done it without you. To Chris White, and Jeff Hall, thanks for believing!

To the staff at La Semana Del Sur, thank you for helping me to publish in Spanish. To Clytie Bunyan and Richard Mize of *The Oklahoman* thanks for taking my project to the next level. To Saundra and Conrad Brown, thanks for your support. To Susan Miller, thanks for being there for me. To Dee Rao, thanks for your Spanish translations. Thanks to Brent Manson for providing comic relief and excellent advice.

I would also like to thank Susan Dees, Wayne Hay, Byron Cato, Scott Nottingham, Ondraye Swanegan, Michael McMillan, Susan Tiffin and the ladies at Eclectix's. If I have forgotten anyone, please forgive me.

— Mi-Ling Stone Poole

Introduction...My Passion

Decorating and writing are two of my passions. My dream of being able to merge the two together was realized when I started writing my weekly decorating columns. My plan was to offer advice to homeowners who had real decorating dilemmas and assist them in finding cost-effective ways to decorate their homes. This was accomplished through my question-and-answer column, *Ask Mi-Ling* and *Mi-Ling's Comfort Zone.*

What I didn't expect was the joy I experienced when people read my columns and laughed out loud, or smiled because they saw themselves in the story. And there is nothing more exciting than the look on clients' faces when they see their newly decorated space for the first time.

When I started this journey I thought I was the one giving the advice, but I soon found out that our home is more than a space—it's our refuge, a place that we can call our own, a space that defines who we are or who we want to be.

With all of the drama and terror that we experience on the outside, we all need a place to call home, a comfort zone. It's not about designer rugs or expensive paintings. It's about providing comfort and a safe haven for our family and friends.

Thank you for allowing me to enter your comfort zone and for helping me to see the real beauty in a home. If you like it, I love it.

Remember, your true calling or passion cannot be measured by a paycheck; it's a feeling you get when something just feels right. You know you have discovered your passion when you would do it for nothing. Trust me I know, because I've been there.

I hope this book and my story encourages you to search for your passion in life. Once you have found it, your life will be full of joy.

Now go out and create your own unique comfort zone!

— Mi-Ling Stone Poole

1

Help! I Need Advice

My Fireplace Is Fire Engine Red

Q: I am in desperate need of some help! We just purchased a house that we are updating. The fireplace is currently painted fire engine red with a high gloss finish. We want to tone this down to a more natural look. Do you have any suggestions as to what we might try? We are at a total loss!

— Cindi A.

A: Removing paint from a fireplace can be a messy proposition, but it can be done. It's fairly easy if the bricks were glazed before they were painted. The glaze would have kept the grout and the grooves in the brick from absorbing the paint. If the bricks are not glazed then you have your work cut out for you. You will need to use a paint stripper to remove the paint.

Purchase a can of KS3 Clean Strip. Apply it with a paint brush, let it cure for 10 minutes and then scrape with a putty knife. You probably won't be able to get all of the paint off completely, but it can still look good because you will get a distressed look.

The other option is to have the face of the bricks sandblasted. If you choose this option, prepare to tape off the rest of the house because you will get a huge amount of dust from this procedure. If all else fails, you can always repaint the fireplace. Try the dry brush technique. You can find out more about dry brushing at your local home improvement store.

A Custom Order Gone Bad

Have you ever ordered a piece of custom furniture, and when the item arrived you were dissatisfied?

When you place a custom order you have to be absolutely sure that you want the product. Some companies have policies that require you to purchase the products even if you are not satisfied with the color or the design. Oftentimes, they will charge you a restocking fee. Therefore, you must be extremely careful and think it through before you place the order.

Here are a couple of suggestions to follow when placing a custom order:

1. Always order a swatch color. Computers and catalogs will not show you the true color of the fabrics. Most companies send swatches free of charge.

2. Measure the item carefully and make sure that it will fit into your design plan and into the proposed space.

3. Once you have determined what you want to order, check other stores in your area before you place the order. I have found special order pieces on the floor at specialty shops.

4. Before you place your order, review the return policy and double check the swatch colors. Make a habit of stapling a piece of the swatch to your receipt. Sometimes a different dye lot will change the color of the order so be sure your swatch will come from that same dye lot.

My Bathroom's Disgusting

Q: My bathroom is decorated with old yellowish-green tile and outdated foil wallpaper. The floor is cream and beige linoleum with gold flecks and it's very worn out. How can I bring my '70s bathroom into the 21st century without replacing the tile? I don't want to spend a lot of money because I'm renting this property. I've asked the landlord for help but he's not interested in assisting me with this project, although he has agreed to let me make the changes.

— Kim from Kansas

A: It sounds like you have your work cut out for you, but there is hope. The first project I would tackle is to remove the old foil wallpaper. Next, texture the walls and paint them a neutral color like taupe or beige. You can opt to remove the old flooring and replace it with a new linoleum floor, or to save money purchase an area rug and put that on the floor instead. Last but not least, clean-up the old tile and add some accessories that will blend in with the tile. You could re-grout the tile to give it a fresh new look. With all that said, I would at least try to get the landlord to pay for the supplies. After all you're providing the labor.

A Leaky Roof Ruined My Carpet

Q: I need help! We recently redecorated our dining room. We painted the walls and added new drapes and new carpeting. However, last week when we had 75 mph winds during a storm our carpet received minor water damage. A leak in our roof soaked the carpet through to the concrete slab. Our dining room is a mess! Do we have to replace the entire carpet?

— S. Anderson

A: I had this happen to me recently and a carpet professional told me to suck up as much of the water as I possibly could with a wet-vac. Next, they instructed me to pull the carpet away from the wall and remove the wet padding. Then, let it dry thoroughly under a fan for several days. Before you put it back into place, have it cleaned professionally and replace the wet pad. If the damage was severe you might have to replace the entire carpet. When in doubt contact your local carpet cleaner or installer and ask for assistance.

Don't forget to repair your leaky roof or you'll be repeating these steps later on down the road. Good luck with the project.

Help! I Just Bought A New Home

Q: I have purchased a new house and noticed that black kitchen tables are in. I have a pine set and wanted to paint it black. Is this possible? What would I use on it, if it is?

One more thing; My bedroom is done in black and off-white toile. What would be a good color for my walls to be? The home I am purchasing has very pale yellow walls and everyone tells me to leave them. What do you think?

— Staci

A: Black kitchen tables are in. Hooker has a beautiful line that includes both dark and light wood tones. You might want to visit your local furniture store to get a few ideas before painting your table.

You will need to sand and prime the table first and then apply a water-based paint. After the paint dries, apply a couple of clear coats of varnish. I would use a dull finish for the varnish. Contact your local home improvement store for more detailed information on what type of paint you should use for the finish on your table.

As far as the yellow walls go, black-and-white toile will work well with yellow, red or pink. You should probably give it a try in your new room before painting it and you might be able to save some money.

I Need More Storage In My Living Room

Q: I want to redecorate my living room, which is small. What would be a good color to make the room look larger? Also, I have three windows all together and would like to do a nice window treatment and still be able to have a lot of light come through the windows.

— R. Handley

A: If you want your living room to appear more spacious, consider painting the ceiling a lighter color than the walls. Apply a light taupe or warm beige color in a shade lighter for the ceiling. Using pale green paint is another option and it will give the room a fresh and cool feeling.

When planning your space try using a few large pieces of furniture or accessories to give the room a grand feel. For example, use chunky curtain rods and finials with your drapes. Mount the drapery panels at the top of the wall close to the ceiling because this will make the window appear taller. Place panels on either side of the windows and use bamboo shades or wood blinds to control the light. This will allow you to take advantage of the light without obstructing the view.

You can also place an oversized couch and large-scaled picture frames on the walls. Keep the coffee table and side tables a little smaller so you have more room to move around.

This Fireplace Is A Mess!

Q: We are redecorating our outdated home and have run into a road block in the living room. The central focal point is a stone fireplace complete with what my mother-in-law thinks is a very valuable stone etching. The picture does not match our décor, and neither does the color of the entire fireplace. How can I change the color of the fireplace and hide the picture without destroying it?

— Carla C.

A: This sounds like a sticky situation. If your mother-in-law is correct, you do not want to damage this fireplace mantel before you have it appraised. I would contact several antique dealers and have it appraised before you go any further. After you've completed that task you have two options.

1. Remove it, sell it, and construct a new one.

2. Keep the existing fireplace and have it professionally cleaned and brought back to its original beauty. If it's not valuable you can even paint it!

The choice is yours, but I would make every effort to work with the existing fireplace. Try to blend it into your décor. After it has been restored it will be a unique focal point in your home and an interesting conversation piece. Do some research and find out more about the etchings and the builder.

Help Me Avoid A Plaster Disaster

Q: I have an old house with plaster walls that I would like to retexture and paint. How do I prepare the walls for retexturing?

Thank you for any direction you can give a style stooge like me.

— Marcus

A: You need to prep the walls prior to retexturing or repainting.

I have listed two suggestions for you to consider.

1. If you are painting over walls that have already been textured and painted, then all you need to do is repair the chipped walls and repaint over the existing paint.

2. If you are re-plastering the wall you will need to prime it with a water-based primer and then retexture and paint. This will allow the new texture to adhere to the existing plaster.

My Ugly Linoleum Floor

Q: My husband and I are renting a house that has horrific linoleum in the entryway and in the kitchen. We can do whatever we want, however, we don't want to invest a lot of money into a rent house. What is an inexpensive way to cover this awful eyesore?

— A. Voight

A: A couple of things come to mind. First of all, I would ask the landlord to buy the products and let him know that you will do the work or hire a professional to do the job. After all, it will bring up the value of his property, not yours. Or maybe you can get him to deduct the supplies from your rent.

I would consider pulling up the old flooring and putting down a new floor. You can use linoleum tile-like squares. The squares are easy to use and you just simply peel and stick. Check out your local home improvement store for more information on linoleum flooring. There are lots of styles, patterns and colors to choose from.

Fabric Walls Are An Alternative To Paint

Q: I just moved into a new apartment with the typical white walls. I have a white leather sofa and couch. Painting is out of the question as far as the management is concerned.

I've heard and seen, on TV a few years back, a technique using designer fabric and liquid starch to cover the walls. I would like your take on this technique, i.e., level of difficulty, how well it stays on the walls and the cost and the condition of the walls when it's removed.

I would very much appreciate a response from you as I would like to know what I'm getting into before I tackle this project.

— Clarese B.

A: I'm not sure about the clean-up of the liquid starch. You might have to do some scraping to get if off of the wall. You might want to consider stapling or tacking fabric to the walls. You could also hang fabric or curtains from a pole. This will give you the color and softness that you want without a lot of clean-up. If you want to create pleats, buy triple the amount of fabric compared to the width of the wall. To clean the fabric, vacuum or dry clean.

Create A Focal Point With Your Fireplace Mantel

Q: My fireplace mantel lacks interest in the living room. Can you give me some advice on how to make it more of a focal point?

— Greg

A: Decorating your fireplace is the perfect way to create a focal point in your living room, and a large mantel is the ideal surface to display your treasured items. Candlesticks, floral arrangements and art work are sure winners when planning your design. You can lean the artwork against the wall and change out pieces on a regular basis.

The main thing to remember about decorating a fireplace is to vary the heights of the decorative pieces that you are displaying. Although the trend has been to add several items to the mantel such as beautiful screens, fireplace tools and books, you might want to consider a minimalist look. A sparsely decorated mantel can be just as beautiful if your fireplace is flanked with beautiful granite, stone or wood. This can be accomplished by adding a vase with one flower or a large mirror that reflects something pretty in the room.

Drop Ceiling Dilemma

Q: Here's my dilemma. We just purchased our first home about a year ago, and the owners before us put in drop ceilings (yuck!). I took it down in our spare bedroom, but it was a huge nightmare. Dust and insulation were everywhere and there was drywall in the carpet, and on the ceiling. It was not in the best of condition. Can you think of any way for me to update my drop ceiling in the living room without making it look lower than it already is? I would be forever grateful!

— Cassi

A: Looking at this question from a design standpoint I would paint the ceiling a lighter color than the walls, which would create the look of a higher ceiling. The other option is to remove the ceiling and totally redo it. You might want to ask yourself a few questions before taking on this project.

1. How long do you plan to live in this house?

2. Are you replacing the carpet?

If you are planning on staying in your new home for more than five years, you might consider replacing the ceiling. If you plan to replace the carpet within the next few years, you should probably replace the ceiling now. As you know, tearing down a suspended ceiling is a messy undertaking and you should take precautions. Wear a jumpsuit and a mask to protect against the dust and debris. You could be removing a couple of year's worth of dust and debris from the ceiling. As always, I strongly suggest that you consult with a professional before you begin the project.

My Cabinets Have Water Damage

Q: I have a house that was built about 15 years ago. It has medium dark oak trim throughout the house. The problem is that some of the master bathroom cabinets have water damage. I need to decide if I should strip and refinish them in the same oak or try a whitewash or just paint them. The walls have wallpaper with a dark red, green, and almond print. The trim and doors in the bath are in the same medium dark oak color. Not all the cabinets are damaged. In fact the over-the-john cabinet is in good shape. I hope you can give me some advice on the direction I should take.

— F. Armstrong

A: It sounds like you already know what you want to do. If you want to keep the existing wallpaper, you can pull the almond color out of the paper and whitewash that color onto your cabinets. If you don't like the wallpaper you should consider changing it now. It doesn't cost that much and it will affect the overall feel of the room. Don't be too concerned about matching the rest of the house with the same color trim. You can paint all of the trim to match the cabinets or leave it alone and just paint the cabinets.

My Living Room Is A Cave

Q: I have a new-for-me older home. The living room is a large rectangle with a fireplace wall and built-in cabinets. The walls have wainscoting at the bottom, then early American wallpaper at the top. The room has one window on the east and one door to the outside on the west and one doorway with swinging doors through to the kitchen. My problem is that I cannot clearly visualize what to do with the wallpapered portion of the living room. The current paper is definitely dated. My cousin tried to help by placing paint chips around two of the doorways, but I still don't "see" what I need to do. The room is dark in general.

— L. Justice

A: It sounds like you're having a problem with the room being too dark. It also seems like the narrowness of the room is closing in on you. I would suggest that you use a striped wallpaper pattern in a light color on the top portion of the wall. Most wallpaper stores will give you a large enough sample that you can take home and tape to the wall to see if you like it. The wide stripes will give the room a more open feel. Consider removing the swinging doors that lead into your kitchen because you may be able to gain additional natural light from an existing window.

I Need Help Selecting My Drape Color!

Q: My husband and I have been remodeling our living room for six-months. We have retextured and painted the walls, replaced our carpeting and bought new living room furniture. I have wanted to replace the drapes but I cannot decide on a color. Our wall color is a light brown linen color. The carpeting is a silver sage. Our furniture is a khaki-gold background with small cabernet and orange-bronze flowers with silver sage and moss leaves. (The orange-bronze flowers are smaller than the cabernet flowers. I know it sounds hideous but it is really nice. The fabric is from the Eddie Bauer motion furniture collection).

My husband thinks we should get a linen color drape to match the walls. I am thinking either silver cabernet or a green color, either the silver sage or maybe a slightly darker green color that would complement the silver sage carpeting. The accents in the room are gold, green and cabernet. What color drape should I choose?

— Lou Ann L.

A: Without seeing an actual photo of your room it's a little difficult to select an exact color. However, I would probably use a neutral color. I think a cream drape with highlights of orange cabernet and sage would work well in that space. You can usually find that type of blend in a raw silk. Another option is to go with a khaki color and then add fringe, beads, or tassels to pull in all of the colors.

If you select a neutral color you might be able to extend the life of your drapes long after you tire of the color scheme.

Are Round Tables In?

Q: I have a dining room that is 14 by 14 feet and I have noticed a lot of large round tables in show homes. I like to entertain and would like to be able to seat at least 10 people. What are your thoughts on this space? What size and shape table would look best in a square room and also allow seating for 10?

— Barbara M.

A: A round dining table should fit well in this space. However, you should take a few things into consideration before you purchase this size table.

1. Do you have a large china hutch or cabinet to display? If so, you might need to use a rectangular table to fit everything in the space.

2. What size are your dining chairs? Armless chairs will allow for more seating.

I have a 48-inch round table in my breakfast room and it seats 4-6 people comfortably. In my formal dining room I placed a 110-inch table and it seats 8-10 people with ease.

Round tables encourage conversations among guests. You will probably need a 60-90-inch round table to accommodate 8-10 guests. You can also use two 48-inch tables. Placing two tables side by side will create an interesting atmosphere for your guests and when you're not using the second table it can be utilized for serving refreshments.

My RV Needs Help

Q: My husband and I recently purchased a 1975 RV. The whole inside is in desperate need of remodeling. But, my biggest problem is the bedding. There are 7 different sizes of foam pieces ranging from 23 inches long to 15 inches wide. The issue I'm coming across is the cost of foam and covering. The foam is expensive to replace and tapestry to cover the bedding runs up to $25 per yard. I prefer replacing the covering with a thick but soft durable material. The foam cannot be salvaged unless you know how to wash a lot of foam. Do you have any suggestions on how we can redo them inexpensively?

This is our starter RV and I really do not want to pour too much money into it. But, I would like to make it cozy for a family of 5 ranging from 3 years to 16 years. Any suggestions would be greatly appreciated.

— Tammy M.

A: I would purchase new foam. You can wash the existing foam with a garden hose and mild detergent, however, it takes quite a while for it to dry and it might be easier to just purchase new foam. You can also find good quality heavy duty fabric on sale at most fabric stores. Consider mixing and matching patterns because that will give you a little more flexibility and it could save you money.

Help! My Home Office Is A Mess

Q: My home office is filled with reference books, two computers, a drawing table, one file cabinet, a book shelf and lots of other stuff. I need to make this space into a functional working environment for my home business. Help!

— V. Driver

A: Sounds like you have a mess! The first thing I would do is take everything out of your office and start cleaning things out.

An easy way to do this is to sort and purge your files of everything that you don't need. Store your tax and old business documents in a waterproof file cabinet and place them on a shelf in your garage or in the closet of your home office.

Find three large boxes and label them. (1.) To keep (2.) To throw away and (3.) To donate. After you finish sorting all of your items you should be able to effectively get everything back in your home office with room to spare. If you're looking for more space, utilize the walls by attaching a few shelves.

Consider office furniture with a dual purpose. Look for furniture that offers plenty of storage and drawer space. You can also use benches with lift-up storage that also can be used for seating your clients. You might want to have a few folding chairs hidden away for quick and easy seating as well. This should solve most of your problems.

I Want My Living Room Back

Q: My living room also serves as a family room for my children. Originally, I had an off-white couch and a wood table in this space and I encouraged my kids to take off their shoes and not to eat in this room. Despite my requests the room still stays a mess most of the time. I realize that this is the only space that they have to watch television and play video games in, but it is also the entry into my home.

What can I do to get my living room back from my kids and still give them a place to hang out?

— Tonia S.

A: It sounds like you're having a difficult time getting your children to pick up after themselves. To make matters worse when you walk in the front door you're constantly reminded of the mess that they're making of your living/family room. In all fairness to the children, they need a place to just chill out and relax. However, don't confuse the issues here. They still need to keep things neat and clean.

I would suggest slip covering your furniture with a washable cotton fabric. To provide storage for their belongings you might want to stack a few wicker baskets in the corner. You won't have to worry about water stains if you add a glass table to the space. I would also add a large throw rug in a dark color that won't show stains and a few throw pillows to keep them off the furniture. After all of these changes you should be able to let the kids go in their new space.

I Can't See My Walls For The Smoke Inside

Q: My fiancé and I currently rent so my walls are painted a nice shade of (what other color) "WHITE." My fiancé and I both smoke. He is disabled so he is home most of the time and he smokes heavily. We have friends and family over frequently and they all smoke as well, contributing to the problem. The top half of my walls are now a nice cream (brown) color from the smoke and the bottoms are still white and we haven't even lived in the house for a year yet. I want to re-paint because I am tired of looking at the two-tone walls. Right now, I am using bleach and water solution in a spray bottle and a sponge mop to clean the walls but what I really want is to paint, using a paint that will wipe down easily with just plain water or a cleanser that is not as harsh as bleach. I want to know what kind of paint you recommend. I know the best solution to my problem would be to quit smoking but I really don't see that happening anytime in the near future. We are probably going to be in this house for a while longer and I would hate to see what the walls would look like if I don't do something about them now.

Any suggestions would be greatly appreciated.

— Katrina

A: Yes, quitting smoking would be a good idea. However, I know that it won't solve your current problem. Here are a few suggestions to get you started.

1. Clean the walls with a product called (TSP) Trisodium phosphate. (You need to use rubber gloves and a mask when applying this product.)

2. When you re-paint the walls use a washable paint.

3. Install a room purifier to keep the house clean and encourage your guests to smoke outside.

For more information on TSP contact a paint store in your area.

2

Decorating Styles

Tips On Adding An African Theme To Your Home

Q: Can you give me any suggestions on how to create an African-themed room with original African textiles and accessories? I don't want the room to feel to over done.

— K. Stone

A: When you merge an exotic theme into your home, you create a totally new and exciting environment. You are only limited by your imagination. It can be both educational and heartwarming to bring your family's heritage into your living space.

When planning an African-themed room you should consider adding authentic decorative African art and textiles. You might want to consider adding printed cloth with earth tones. These vibrant colors mimic the rich and colorful heritage of Africa.

Kente is an African textile woven into a cloth that can be used to make throws, wall hangings, pillows, tablecloths, and bed spreads. You can also purchase the textile to re-cover your existing furniture.

Harriet B. Schiffer, Ph.D. and an African art and clothing specialist, said the origins of Kente cloth lie within the ancient tradition of narrow strip weaving found in the Western Sudan dating back to the 11th century, and further back to the Nile River over 2,000 years ago. Kente, as we know it, dates back to the 17th century and the Asante people of Ghana in West Africa where richly colored, intricately woven ceremonial cloths were exclusively created to be worn by kings, queen mothers and chiefs. "Kente cloth merges fashion with afro-centric philosophy," Schiffer told me. There are seven traditional colors used in Kente cloth.

- **Yellow** is associated with the yolk of an egg and edible fruit. It symbolizes sanctity, preciousness, spiritual vitality and fertility.

- **Red** is associated with blood. Red is used as a symbol of heightened spirituality and of sacrifice and struggle.

- **Green** is associated with planting and harvesting. It symbolizes growth, vitality, health and spiritual rejuvenation.

- **Purple** is used in rituals and healing. Purple cloths are mostly worn by women.

- **Maroon** has a close resemblance to clay, therefore it is associated with healing and the power to repel malevolent spirits.

- **Gold** is associated with gold nuggets and therefore is associated with royalty wealth and high status.

- **Black** derives its significance from the notion that new things get darker as they mature. It symbolizes communion with ancestral spirits and antiquity.

You can incorporate a unique design and a conversation piece into your home by using Kente cloth.

Create A Home Design With Paris In Mind

Are you looking for a design style with glitz, glamour and lots of ambience? Maybe you want to bring a little romance back into your life. If so, consider decorating a room in your home around a Paris theme. Bedrooms, bathrooms and entryways will come alive when you add a little bit of Paris to the room.

Over the past few years the trend has been to buy Paris accessories with "Paris" written on them, or architectural items such as the Eiffel Tower and display them in your space. Pink, red and black-and-white are all strong colors that have been associated with French décor. For a softer feel try using use yellow and blue.

If this is a little too much for your taste, create your own Paris style by first deciding what Paris means to you. Paris is known for fashion and food. When I hear the name it reminds me of not only Paris Hilton, but a runway filled with beautiful fashion models wearing the best and most outrageous couture designs. Wine, French bread and cheese are the foods that I think about most when Paris comes to mind, but let us not forget the wonderful French pastries that Paris is known for as well. One of the most prominent images of Paris is an open-air café and a good bottle of French wine.

Paris also reminds me of trendy handbags and fabulous shoes. Paris décor is like old furniture that's appreciated for its value and tables and chairs that show wear and tear from generations of use.

Now, let's take your view or meaning of Paris and transform it into a design that speaks to your heart and soul. Here are a few ideas to get you started.

1. If it's the fashion that makes your heart sing place beautiful designer shoes on shelves along with unusual purses and hats to make a fashion statement in your bedroom or walk-in closet. Frame and display large posters of runway models on the wall.

2. Do gardens come to mind in your vision of Paris? If so, display prints with landscapes and beautiful flowers. You can even purchase wallpaper with a French garden theme.

3. The architecture of Paris is world-renowned and to get that vibe in your room use black-and-white photos of Paris landmarks or purchase an old map of France and decoupage it to an antique trunk or frame it and hang it on the wall.

4. Food can also be very inspirational. Take photos of French bread or baguettes. Display colorful photographs of wine cheese and fruit around your kitchen. Purchase a small café table for your kitchen or sunroom and drape it with a beautiful French table cloth to add ambience to your room.

Paris accessories are readily available and you can choose from signs, prints, towels, vases, wall hangings and even black-and-white photos of coffee shops.

Discover your meaning of Paris and transform it into a new design space just for you and your family by using a little imagination and some accessories that you might already have around the house.

Get The Feel Of A Bed And Breakfast In Your Home

Would you like to create the feel of a bed and breakfast in your home?

When you consider decorating your home to resemble a B&B you should first decide what type of ambience you want to create before you begin.

Here are a couple of themes you might want to include in your home.

Romantic honeymoon theme-This can be achieved by adding large fluffy robes to hooks in your bathroom. Use lots of fresh flowers and roses throughout the home. Add soft and elegant fabrics like satins and silks to add romance and, of course, a crystal chandelier.

Spa and retreat theme-Concentrate on sprucing up the bathrooms. Add oversized tubs and double showers with natural stone to your bathroom area. You might want to create a room just for meditation. The key to this style is total relaxation and pampering. Keep lots of bubble bath and oils on hand and stock your bathroom with sweet-smelling skin care products. You might want to invest in a massage chair and place it in the corner of the room and light candles that enhance relaxation.

Country cottage theme-Add plaid and floral fabrics for a country theme. If you have an outdoor porch, dress it up and add rocking chairs, swings and lots of country folk-art. Go to the antique stores and buy old pottery and appliances to give your home the feel of an old country cottage.

Victorian theme-Create a parlor for family gatherings. Use antique furniture and reupholster it to add an authentic look. Use vibrant colors from the Victorian era. Add lots of chandeliers and light fixtures to add drama. Apply Victorian-styled wallpaper throughout your home to blend in with the theme. Coat your walls with traditional Victorian paint colors.

Nostalgic theme-If your home is located near a historic area you might want to consider blending the décor with that era. For example if you are near an old railroad station consider adding a train room or other nostalgic theme to create the feeling that you have checked in at an inn.

Whichever theme you choose, all of the rooms should exude a feeling of comfort. Anything is possible and it's only limited by your imagination.

This Bathroom Is Clowning Around

Q: In my granddaughter's room I want to do her bathroom in a clown motif. If the shower curtain I purchased is in primary colors with white-faced clowns on it and the current walls are off-white what colors do you suggest for the walls in the bathroom? I believe the bathroom is a Hollywood style. Could the two sections be in two different colors?

— B. Harrison

A: It sounds like your granddaughter will have a lot of fun in her new clown bathroom. You didn't say if the room on the other side is a guest bedroom or another child's room so I'll assume that it's an empty guest bedroom. I would paint the walls a warm yellow color and accent with primary colors.

Go out and purchase some cute clowns to place around the room and up on the shelves you can also use clown accessories for the soap and tooth brush dispensers. Buy her lots of colorful towels in red, blue, yellow, green and orange. It will be an investment because after she grows tired of the clowns you can use them in another bathroom or in a different design.

Take The Wow Test On Holiday Décor

Is your home ready for the holidays? Do you have clever decorations, interesting art work or a beautiful rug in your entryway? If you're planning to have company for the festivities ahead take the "wow" test. If you fail, you still have time to get your humble abode in shape with these quick and easy tips.

Step outside of your home and open the front door. Look around and up and down as if you were visiting your home for the first time. Is there anything that appeals to your eye? Do you have bold colors, a great piece of furniture, a beautiful rug or floral arrangement that begs you to enter?

The most welcoming homes are ones that utilize all of your senses. When you open the door you should hear great holiday music, smell fragrant berries or flowers and see something spectacular and unusual with lots of color. This is the "wow" factor.

Here are some tips to "wow" your guests for the holidays.

1. Use luxurious and bold-colored drapes with heavy poles in an unusual place. Try the hallway or simply hang them on a wall without windows.

2. Add a beautiful chandelier to your entry. Shop at thrift stores and have old lights re-wired, put on new shades and "wow."

3. Do you love music? Invest in a baby grand piano and you'll "wow" your guests when they open the front door. A player piano will add to the ambience of the room as well.

4. Short on funds? No problem, pull out all the stops by adding candles. It doesn't matter if they are large, small, tall or thin, just place them around your home and be sure that the scents coming from the candles are similar.

Most of my clients want the "wow" factor. They want their guests to feel welcome, entertained and comfortable. I try to accomplish this by utilizing unusual items or bold colors. For the holidays, pull out beaded and colorful pillows and place them around your home and even in the entryway.

Don't be afraid to go over the top. It's all about glamour and casual elegance.

If you need color on a budget just open the refrigerator and grab some apples, pears, lemons and berries. All of these items will "wow" your guests if displayed properly. Just find a large vase or bowl and arrange them any way you desire. For a little punch of color, just place water in your vase and empty several bags of fresh berries into it. For drama use a floating candle or a bunch of flowers and you're set for the holidays.

If you failed the "wow" test don't panic. You still have time to get it all together. Now go out and create your own unique comfort zone and "wow" them with your creativity.

3

Mixing Colors & Patterns

Animal Prints Gone Wild

Q: I have my whole house done in "safari," lots of black, browns, animal prints, maps of Africa, old trunks, etc. When someone comes over, I always say, "Welcome to the jungle." I love the safari look, but my daughter tells me it's a little wild. Do you have any suggestions that could be added to my jungle to tame it down? I would like something that would blend with what I already have.

— Lee Ann

A: Sometimes when we're decorating we have a tendency to take a theme to the extreme and then we get tired of it rather quickly. This might be the case with your animal print room.

I would incorporate floral-printed pillows and throws with hues of sage green, wine or red.

Exchange some of your animal print pictures with pictures of flowers or landscapes with flowers. This should tone things down quite a bit.

To add additional drama, hang some floral drapes in the living room. All of these additions should change the entire look of your room.

Who Made Those Drapes?

Q: A couple months ago I read your column about a breakfast room. I think it was yours. Could you please let me know where you got the pattern or who made the little curtains you had in the room? They were double-sided and they folded over at the top and were hung from the rods with ring clips. I have just had a room added to my house that is all windows and they would be perfect. Thanks for your help!

— S. Anderson

A: That breakfast room was a real challenge for me. I was fortunate to find fabric that matched the seat cushions on my dining set. I bought the material from Fabrics Unlimited in Oklahoma City. What we did was basically line one side of the drapes with the check pattern and the other side with a wheat-colored fabric. So you can un-clip them and turn them around and fold the flap over and have a totally new curtain. As far as the design goes, I tore a couple of pictures of curtains that I liked out of a magazine and sketched a pattern that merged the two. Susan Dees of Fabric Unlimited had them made in her workshop. The wrought-iron poles and clips were pur-chased there as well. I get tired of things rather quickly so this was a good option for me.

What Do Colors Really Mean?

Q: I heard you on the radio sometime in December and you all were talking about colors. I was on my way to work and did not get to write down what all you had said about the different colors and what moods they bring out. What are the best colors to use in a master bedroom, living room and kitchen?

— Misty

A: Color selection is one of the most important elements of a design project. Colors have been proven to affect us psychologically and the proper selection will assure a pleasant design.

You need to base your decision on how each particular color makes you feel and the mood that you are trying to create in your room.

Are you looking for a kitchen that exudes warmth? If so, pick colors that are warm and cozy such as oranges and reds.

If you are longing for a spa retreat in your master bedroom and bath, paint it celery green or a warm beige or soft yellow.

For a relaxing and warm family room, consider a dark chocolate brown and add a splash of turquoise for an updated look.

If you don't have a clue which colors you prefer, go to your closet and pick out your favorite dress or tie and use that color.

Rental Homes Need Color Too

Q: Owning a home, you have many ways to spice up the walls with color and designs, yet when renting an apartment you're limited to painting the walls. How much art, frames, or fixtures can you nail in the walls? With bland creamish-beige walls what can one do without paint? I would love ideas to make my apartment feel like home.

— A. Akhtar

A: First of all ask your landlord if he will allow you to make improvements. Oftentimes, if the colors are not too bold the landlord will give you permission to paint. You might want to consider just painting one wall in a bold color. That will help break up the bland feeling of the room and you'll only have one wall to repaint when you move out. As far as pictures go, I would use small nails and just patch them with a little filler upon your departure. You can also lean large pictures against the wall for a splash of color or incorporate a folding screen into your space for interest. Drapes are always an option and most rental properties already have the poles in place, so all you have to do is find a colorful pair of curtains.

Should I Paint My Antique Chest?

Q: I recently purchased an antique chest, but I'm not happy with the way it looks. I would like to paint the chest an off-white color. It is currently a dark cherry wood color. If I paint the chest will it decrease the value?

— Rose

A: This is a very good question. A lot of people buy antique pieces that they would like to incorporate into their décor. Oftentimes, they are paralyzed by the decision to change the piece or to leave it as is. This is usually based on the fear that changing the finish will decrease the value of the furniture. If you are purchasing the piece to resell as an antique collectible, I would hesitate before I would change the finish. Contact an antique dealer and have your new chest appraised.

After you have had it appraised you can make an educated decision on how you want to proceed. If you are not concerned about the value and you would like to utilize it as a new piece of furniture go ahead and change the finish.

Color Washing Wood Paneling

Q: I have wood paneling on my living room walls. I am considering painting them but I would like to be able to paint and texture without ruining the wood paneling. What would be the best way to do this?

— Kristi C.

A: Wood paneling has been used for years to both protect the walls from damage in high-traffic areas and to add warmth and texture to a room. I will assume that your wood is a dark color. You stated that you would like to change the color but you don't want to damage the wood, just in case you want to go back to utilizing it at a later date. That statement makes me think that you like the style of the wood, but not the color.

You might want to consider color washing the panels. This will allow the wood grain to shine through and will give you a color change. You can use a transparent stain or you can use two different colors in an oil-based paint. Usually it's a light and a dark paint color combination. You will need to thin the oil-based paint with mineral spirits. Usually each can is thinned 50:50. I strongly suggest you contact your local paint store or home improvement center and ask a professional for details on how to color wash wood paneling.

Can I Use Animal Prints With My New Couch?

Q: I received some almost-new furniture from my grandmother and it's beautiful and very comfortable, but it does not go with my living room décor. I have animal prints in the living room and the couch is a red/cream plaid, with accent pillows in large flowers of the same colors. It also has some green in it, but not dominant. The matching chair is the same as the accent pillows, large flowers. I love the furniture and would like to decorate my living room to go with it. Any suggestions?

— Brandy H.

A: I have found that florals and leopard prints work well together. I'm not sure if you have leopard, zebra or something else, but here's a tip on mixing and matching patterns. If you have the same color tones you can mix and match the patterns…it just takes a little courage. You don't want the patterns to fight with one another. They should complement each other. Try using a small, medium and large pattern in your design. You can add a solid green or cream pillow and accent with your animal prints. Find three colors that you like and use them consistently.

What Colors Look Good With Pine Furniture?

Q: I am looking into painting my bedroom walls. I have pine furniture with black wrought-iron accents. I want to paint my walls in a suede finish. Would this look OK? I'm changing linens to match whatever color I decide. Are there any color tones that would go better with the pine furniture?

— Keri C.

A: I wouldn't try to match my color scheme with the pine furniture. You should select a color palette that you like and choose from those colors. It really depends on the type of mood that you are trying to create in your space. If you mix blue and white fabrics together, or yellow and blue, you will create a cool and breezy atmosphere in your bedroom. For a more sophisticated and tailored look, consider using black-and-white or red and white.

If you are applying a suede finish to the walls, try a captivating color like tobacco and accent with white or black.

Adding Pizzazz To Tiny Bathrooms

Q: I have two half-baths with a full shower in between with doors separating these small areas. They are painted off-white and I would like to change that.

What colors would you suggest? The floors have 12-inch tiles and are a beige color. I have silver and black frames on the wall. I am a 45-year old male and I lean toward a contemporary look. Thanks for your time.

— Randy

A: It sounds like you have a Jack and Jill bathroom with connecting doors. This type of bathroom design can be very challenging, because you have to consider the décor of each room on either side of the bathroom before you begin your project.

You didn't tell me what the color scheme is in the other rooms so I'll just use something neutral.

If you want to stay with the contemporary concept, you might want to try painting wide stripes of taupe and cream on the walls. This will give you the contemporary look with a little pizzazz and it will open up the space.

After you finish painting you should be able to add new red accents and keep the silver and black frames in place on the wall.

4

Decorating Ideas To Ponder

Furniture Arrangement Is Key To Successful Design

Q: My husband has given me the OK to redecorate my living room. It is a large rectangle with only one wall available for the wall unit/media center. There are several windows on one end and a fireplace with a large carved mantle and shelves on the other end of the room. I have a leather sofa and leather chair with ottoman, which will stay. I want two matching chairs with a print to brighten up the solidness of the leather. I have trouble arranging pieces. My arranging leaves the room feeling boring or not put together correctly. If someone were to put it together for me, that would be the ultimate, but not practical. I don't know what to do. What do you suggest?

— Lisa H.

A: Since you have a long and narrow space, divide it into two unique spaces. I would place two oversized comfortable chairs with bold prints at the end of the room that houses the shelving. This will allow you to create a library or reading area and display art and books on the shelves. On the other end of the room in front of the fireplace, pull your sofa and chair close together. Add a coffee table and lots of accessories to cozy both spaces up. You now have two defined living areas within one room. When accessorizing, blend in the pillows from the chairs with the leather sofa and place leather pillows on the oversized chairs. Use rugs with similar textures and colors to ground the spaces together.

My Table Needs Help

Q: I am having trouble decorating the tables in my living room. I have a square coffee table in front of my sofa and a round table covered in fabric next to a large chair and ottoman. What can I place on these tables without them looking overdone and cluttered? How much is too much?

Thanks for your help!

— Sidney

A: Putting the final touches on your tables can seem a bit overwhelming at times. Don't make it harder then it really is. Place things on your table that you love to look at and that serve a function. Don't worry about it being too cluttered.

Consider stacking a few hardbound books on a topic that you enjoy. Maybe it's a photo book of your favorite entertainer, design books or sports memorabilia. Next, try crystal vases or containers that can hold nuts or candy. Crystal is a great light reflector. You can also drape a sample of your favorite fabric on the table, or a strand of colorful beads.

Select a beautiful box to hold all of your remotes for your entertainment center. Mix in a few candlestick holders with decorative candles; these will come in handy if you have a sudden power outage.

Use your imagination and have fun creating your new table-scapes. Surround yourself with items that have sentimental value or that have a purpose.

Mirrors Can Add Depth And Ambience To A Room

Q: I love to have a lot of mirrors in my house, but would like some creative ways to use and show them off. Do you have any ideas?

— Barbara

A: Mirrors are great accessories to have in your home. I always place a mirror near my front and back doors so I can check out how I look before I answer the door or leave the house. In a small room a mirror can add depth and open up the space if placed in the proper location. Position your mirror on the wall opposite something beautiful that you would like to reflect.

For wall art, try grouping small mirrors together that have a variety of frames and shapes. This will give your room a dramatic look.

To dress up a dining table, use your framed mirror in place of a tray, and then add crystal and candles to create a romantic ambience.

Mirrors come in a variety of colors, shapes and sizes and frames are available in almost every finish imaginable from faux leopard to polka dots.

Whether you select a beveled mirror or an antique piece the right choice can add function and character to your décor.

Selecting Carpet, Tile And Paint Can Be Mind Boggling

Q: My husband and I are building a house. We're actually doing a lot of the work ourselves. We're getting close to the point of painting and putting down carpet and tile. (Let me say first that I know that we should paint the walls before putting down the carpet). Here is my question: Would it be easier to find my carpet color first, then my paint color, or find my paint color, then my carpet color? I have some ideas about the colors I want to use. The house will be primarily earth tones with splashes of colors. I am just a little confused on how I should go about finding my carpet and paint.

— Angie G.

A: First, select a variety of tile, rug and paint samples for the room. Most tile and carpet stores will allow you to check out samples. Paint samples are readily available and they even give you the lighter and darker tones together on the card. Place all of your selections on the floor in your room. Mix and match the various options. Try not to match them perfectly, since contrast will add to the style and décor of your home. Choose neutral colors for your tile and carpet and then you can change the wall color on a whim. Assess the lighting in the room first, because it could affect the appearance of the colors.

The Upside And Downside Of Wallpaper

Are you ready for a change in your décor this spring? If so, you might want to consider adding wallpaper to one of your rooms.

Here's the upside to wallpapering:

The wide variety of wall covering that is available will boggle your mind. You can easily change the color and attitude of any room with your selection. If you want a room with orange, you can have it. If you're in the Red Hat Society, you can have a wall full of red hats and shoes. The sky is the limit.

After the wall covering has been applied you can choose from a variety of accessories donned with the same patterns. Wallpaper manufacturers have developed complementary colors and accessories that coordinate with the wallpaper patterns. You can find lampshade, fabrics and pillows to name a few.

The downside to wallpapering:

Taking the wallpaper down can be a bit difficult if you are not familiar with the products. It's fairly easy to pull down the wall covering but after it's been taken down you need to decide if you want to leave the glue in place and use a liner and paint over it or if you want to go through the long process of scraping off the glue to get a clean surface upon which to work.

You need to decide early on if you want to use a wallpaper liner. If applied properly you can paint over the product. Oftentimes, you can texture right over the glue after you run a test. If you apply the texture and it doesn't bubble, it should be OK.

Tips for taking down wallpaper:

1. You can rent a heat gun that will heat up the surface and this equipment will allow you to easily remove the remaining glue.

2. Mix warm water with vinegar and spray onto the wall. Saturate the wall and then scrape with a large metal scraper.

3. Instead of pulling the paper down use a wallpaper liner and paint right over this product.

Whatever you decide to do just keep in mind that when you are selecting your wallpaper make sure that you can live with it for at least 5 years. It will become outdated in most instances and you will need to replace it. Sometimes applying a can of paint might be easier in the long run, but it just depends on how much work you are willing to put into the project.

Storage Is The Key To Creating A Workable Space

Are you planning a new work space? Do you want to design an office, sewing room or just a small place to wrap gifts and pay your bills?

When purchasing furniture for this space, consider all of your options and look for pieces that will also handle your storage needs.

Many popular designers such as Martha Stewart and Christopher Lowell have created furniture specifically to aid the consumer in creating not only a beautiful room but a functional living space. If you can't afford Martha Stewart's Bernhardt line, consider purchasing furniture that you can put together yourself.

Christopher Lowell has designed functional and beautiful office suites that will accommodate all of your storage needs from book shelves to filing cabinets. This added storage helps to keep all of your computer accessories within reach but out of sight.

First, determine the style that you would like to incorporate into your home. You can select from contemporary, traditional, mission, country and even art deco.

However, when selecting these new do-it-yourself products you need to consider the level of skill that it takes to successfully build this furniture. Many of the store clerks will tell you that it's a breeze, but I can tell you from experience that it will take several long hours and maybe a couple of days to put an entire office suite together.

Here are a few tips:

1. Make sure you have the right tools. This should include screw-drivers, hammers and drills. Remember, having the right tool is half the battle.

2. Allow for ample space to construct the unit. You might need to remove other pieces of furniture from the room to give yourself additional space to work.

3. Read the directions thoroughly. Go through each step and then return to step one. This will help you visualize each step. If you skip a step this could ruin the entire project.

4. Never open more than one box at a time. Keep all of the boxes separate and just build one unit at a time.

5. Find a friend to help you. Many of these projects require two people.

6. Be patient. Rome wasn't built in a day.

7. Be realistic. If it becomes too difficult or time consuming, hire someone to put it together for you. Most of the office supply companies have a list of people who specialize is this area.

Creating a comfort zone that is both functional and pleasing to the eye will allow you to work more efficiently in your new space.

Wrap Your Walls In Christmas For The Holidays

Q: I would like to dress up my walls for the holidays but I don't have a lot of money. Do you have any price-saving suggestions or tips for me?

— Lilah R.

A: Here's an easy and inexpensive way to add glamour and a festive mood to your home without breaking the bank.

My friend's husband just came back from L.A. and he said that all of the restaurants are wrapping photos and pictures in beautiful wrapping paper and then placing them back on the walls. It looks like a wall of Christmas gifts.

For a sleek, sophisticated look select silver and gold or red and gold wrapping paper. Be sure to use wide ribbon. When you turn the picture frame over to wrap it, make sure that you don't cover up the hardware needed to reposition the picture on the wall.

Rugs Warm Up A Drab Living Space

Do you feel like your room is missing something? Do you want to add a punch of color to the space or separate two distinctive living areas?

If so, consider adding a new rug to your décor. A properly selected rug will add warmth to your space as well as assist you in defining separate living areas within one room. The colors you select for your rug should blend but not match perfectly. This is one of the best ways to add interest to your design without having to spend a huge amount of money.

A new rug, some pillows and a few accessories will change the entire look and feel of the space in no time.

Here are a few tips that will help you with your rug shopping:

1. Before you make your selection, consider the color palette for your room. It's much easier to take your pillows, drapes and wall color samples to the store, instead of dragging several large rugs to your home. Save that task for the final two selections.

2. Rugs come in a variety of colors, textures and styles. Consider your design style and then select the appropriate rug that fits with that style. You don't want to place a country-styled braided rug in front of a modern leather couch.

3. To save time and a possible headache, fill a notebook with all of your fabric samples and room dimensions and leave it in your car. Then, the next time you're out shopping and you see the perfect rug you'll be better prepared to make a confident decision.

4. Remember, purchasing a rug takes time and a lot of patience. Don't rush it.

Staging Your Home For A Quick Sell

Q: I am about to put my house on the market. I have made tons of improvements and updates, but I would like to know more about how to stage the house for showings. It's priced slightly higher than the majority of homes in the neighborhood due to the updates. I want people to fall in love with the house, and not to be able to imagine themselves living anywhere else. Thanks for your help!

— Merissa

A: It sounds like you've put a lot of thought into updating your home. A word of caution, don't put more money into your home than the market will bear. The first thing you need to do is get rid of the clutter. Put away your family photographs, collectibles and any other items that will distract home buyers. Remove large pieces of furniture, books and other items to give your home a more spacious feel. Clean off your counters and put your portable appliances away.

1. Clean your home from top to bottom, inside and out. Don't forget to clean and organize your closets, pantry, linen closets and kitchen cabinets.

2. Get rid of pet odors and remove your pets during the showings.

3. Replace or clean carpeting and paint your walls a neutral color.

4. Take down busy wallpaper.

5. Remove artificial plants and display fresh flowers and live plants.

Create a comfort zone by baking a batch of cookies. Make a fresh pitcher of lemonade and add a few large lemon slices. Turn on soothing music.

Check your curb appeal. Paint exterior doors, change knobs and plant flowers. Remember, if you can't get them out of the car to see your home you've already lost the battle.

What Type Of Flooring Is Suitable For Wheelchairs?

Q: My husband and I have been in our home for almost 12 years and it is in need of new flooring. He is a paraplegic and we were advised to get either berber or commercial carpet. Would it be in our best interest to get ceramic tile instead or perhaps some type of wooden flooring (Pergo)? If carpet was chosen what would you suggest?

— M. Willis

A: Between the two types of carpeting I would install a thin indoor-outdoor carpet. Berber carpets tend to be thicker and have knots. If you select tile, you need to make sure that the grout lines are small so that you can avoid any accidents. If you use wood you should install a glue-down hardwood floor or a laminate. The glue-down floor is available in natural wood and can be stained to match your décor. Once you apply the finish it will not be as slick as a laminate floor. The key is to make sure that the floor is flush with your other floors.

In order to make the proper selection on your flooring, take your husband to a home improvement center or a tile and flooring showroom where displays are available. Ultimately, he should be the one to make the final decision based on how comfortable and easy it is for him to get around.

Help! My Window Is An Eyesore

Q: We live on a golf course and I have a large picture window in my family room that I need to cover with a drapery or some other kind of window treatment. The main problem is that when the previous owners installed this new window they left the metal frame exposed. The window doesn't match any of my existing windows and the frame runs right down the center of this large picture window.

I would like to replace this window or cover up the frame. Do you have any suggestions as to what I should do?

— Terry

A: Before you address the issue with the window treatments, you might want to fully consider your options for covering up the window frame or even replacing the entire window.

Sometimes homeowners will try to conceal something that is not attractive instead of dealing with the real problem. If you decide not to replace the window and spend hundreds of dollars on new window treatments you might still be disappointed, because when you open the drapes you will still see the ugly frame. You could have a carpenter build you a window frame to hide the metal or you could replace the entire window and get the look you really want. I would select a window that is similar to your existing windows.

Just a thought: I have a sneaking suspicion that the previous window may have been broken out several times from flying golf balls and that's why it was replaced with a lesser quality window.

My Ceiling Needs A Lift

Q: I recently purchased a new home and the only thing I'm concerned about is the low kitchen ceiling. What can I do to make it appear taller? The cabinets are stained in a fruit wood color and they are flush with the ceiling and the walls are teal green.

Do you have any suggestions on how I can visually create a taller ceiling without raising the roof or ripping out the ceiling?

— Rhealene C.

A: First of all, I would suggest that you take a few months to live with your new kitchen and get used to the environment before you start making any drastic changes. Oftentimes, when we move from one home to another we are still carrying around the image of our old kitchen in our memory. It will take some time to get used to your new space.

When you are ready to tackle the project, one of the easiest things you can do is paint your ceiling a lighter color than the wall. This will trick the eye and add "height" to the ceiling.

If you have a window in the kitchen you can raise the curtain rod and create the illusion of a taller window, which will also add more height to the room.

Sometimes the sheen of the paint can make a difference as well.

Here are a few tips that will help you create a visually higher ceiling:

- Use flat paint on the ceiling instead of paint with a high gloss.

- When mixing the paint for the ceiling, mix one quarter of the formula. This will match the wall color but appear a shade or two lighter after it is painted on the ceiling.

- You might also want to consider painting your upper cabinets a lighter color. This would take some of the weight off the top of the room.

I don't know how much redecorating you are planning on doing, but you should take note of the direction and the style of your backsplash. If it's too busy and running horizontally it could be part of the problem. You might want to select something that runs vertically with soft colors.

All of these changes should give your room the lift you desire.

Dress Up Your Windows

Q: I would like to dress up my windows in my home but still have the light shining in. Can you give me any advice on the latest ideas in window treatments?

Thank you for your help.

— Karen M.

A: During the winter months it's important to allow sunlight to filter into your home in order to keep out the cold weather blues. Having grown up in Minnesota, I know a little bit about this disorder, and I have learned to appreciate a good dose of natural light when it's cold outside.

Heavy drapery treatments that block out all of the sunlight can be functional for a bedroom, but can also create a dreary ambience. On the other hand, a vibrant window treatment that allows light to filter through can add a punch of color to an otherwise mundane space.

If you would like to control the natural light more efficiently in your home, you should consider combining drapes with wood blinds or shutters.

During the past few years heavy Italian fabrics have become popular again. But if you don't want to spend $75 or more per yard for an entire wall of window treatments, flanking has become very acceptable. The trend has been to flank each side of your window with a rich panel of fabric. Installing a drapery on each side instead of going across the entire window can save you hundreds of dollars in labor and materials and still enable you to buy the expensive fabrics that you desire.

Indoor awnings are hot this year and they look good in both laundry rooms and kitchens. Not only will they give your space the look of an outdoor café, but with the right fabric selection they will add a bit of whimsy to the space without covering up the entire window.

Take your time and research all of your options before making a final selection. Determine the function of each space and the amount of light that you want to keep in and keep out, before you shell out the big bucks for window treatments.

Border Blues

Q: I am about to redecorate a spare bedroom of a house I've lived in for a couple of years. The former owner had the builder personalize one of the bedrooms and the bathroom next door to it with a decorative wallpaper border at the top of the walls all the way around the room. The border is about 6 to 8 inches wide, which seems huge.

The border does not fit in with my décor, and I can't figure out what to do with it. The bedroom walls are lightly textured, but I don't think the walls are textured under the border. I know there is no texture under the wallpaper in the bathroom. Imagine that!

But even if there is texture under the border in the bedroom, there won't be much left if I remove the border. I don't cherish the thought of retexturing the entire bedroom because of the cost and hassle.

If texturing is the best option, can I texture over the wallpapered border? Can I texture over wallpaper in the bathroom? What do you suggest to remedy my border-wallpaper dilemma?

— J. Lowrey

A: I am a firm believer that you should do a project right the first time so that you don't have to repeat the process later on down the road.

Based on my personal experiences with wallpaper, I would highly recommend removing the old border first and then texturing over the untextured portion of the wall. You should not have to do the entire wall over. After you have your walls prepped, paint them the color of your choice and be done with it.

If you would rather texture over the border, you can purchase a product called Shieldz Primer from your local wallpaper store. Applying a sealer will allow you to texture right over the wallpaper.

Sometimes the hardest decision is to make a decision.

Will Granite Countertops Enhance My Kitchen?

Q: I am thinking about redoing my kitchen and I have been checking into using granite countertops. I recently heard about a new technique that applies the granite directly on to your existing counters. Is it better to tear out my existing countertops or apply an overlay?

— Jeri H.

A: I have installed granite in several of my homes and I must say that after using marble, tile and other solid surfaces, it is one of my all-time favorites for the kitchen. Not only does it add a richness and sophistication to your design, but it is also easy to clean. However, the best reason for utilizing granite is being able to take a hot pan from the oven and place it directly onto the surface without worrying about damaging your countertops.

When you are making a decision on using a granite overlay or a slab you need to take a few things into consideration:

- Granite overlays are usually only ¼ inch thick.

- You normally won't have the same number of color choices and your finished edge choices are limited.

- On a full slab you can choose from a variety of edges which include bull-nose and chiseled.

- You can expect to pay several thousand dollars for a complete countertop redo for an average-sized kitchen or anywhere between $40 to $50 a square foot.

If you are interested in a clean and simple look with a minimal amount of dismantling, then an overlay might be for you.

But if you want a free-flowing piece of granite with custom edges you should consider tearing out your existing countertops and installing granite the old-fashioned way.

Remember, the overlay is only as good as the foundation, so be sure that your countertop surfaces are sturdy.

Design A Room Around Your Passion

Cailey's passion in life is to be a fashion designer. She spends hours a day on her computer designing clothes with her *Barbie* software.

Her parents, Lance and Susan, wanted to encourage and inspire their 12-year-old daughter to reach for her goals and find her true passion by creating a room that would stimulate her interests in fashion design.

They enlisted the help of Cailey's mentor, Tina, to assist them with this project. They drew their inspiration from pictures of clothing and boxes with shoes and dresses on them to give the room the feel of a designer's studio mixed with the glamour of a 1920s film set.

Lance did all of the carpentry work for the space. They decided to keep the entire project a secret from their daughter until the day the project was completed.

Here's what they did:

1. They painted Cailey's walls an off-white color and then washed the corners and edges of the walls in a mustard-colored paint. Then they washed the cracks and corners with black paint mixed with a little brown glaze. This technique gave the walls an aged appearance.

2. To make the canopy bed, Lance created a round wooden box that he attached to the wall. He painted the box black and added a recessed light. This light is perfect for reading in bed and allows Cailey's photograph of a red dress to shine between the drapes that surround her bed.

3. They covered the box with a black toile fabric and glued on trim and then added the drapes. This was a no-sew project and everything was either stapled or glued.

4. Susan worked her magic on an existing pine armoire and sanded it for a distressed look. Then they painted it black, antiqued it and applied a light coat of varnish. For a unique finish to the piece they stapled batting and fabric to the front panels.

To add whimsy to the space, they hot-glued roses to a framed piece of artwork. In another corner of the room they created a reading area with a comfortable chair and a floor lamp. Beside the chair they organized a workspace for Cailey to design her patterns.

The beautiful drapes and valance they made gave the room a grown-up feel.

For additional lighting they reused an old brass chandelier by painting it black and adding crystals for a touch of glamour.

Lance, Susan and Tina created a personal space for Cailey that will encourage her to pursue her dream of becoming a fashion designer.

Fringe Can Add A New Look To Your Furniture

Have you ever wondered how to make your furniture look new without having to buy new fabric and pay an upholstery guy a couple hundred dollars?

If your furniture is still in good condition try using fringe to accent a new color or to add a dramatic look.

After purchasing a new designer rug for my living room, I decided that I had to change something on my sofas in order to help them blend in better with the new rug. These were Bernhardt curved couches that were only a couple of years old.

I suggested to my husband that we should recover the six large detached pillows and it would cost more than $1,000.

Needless to say, he was not interested. So I started to think of what I could do to enhance them without recovering.

I thought I could find just the right size pillows at a discount store but I searched for several months before I gave up on that idea.

One day I was at the fabric store looking for something for one of my clients when I saw this beautiful fringe. It was perfect.

Here's what I did:

1. Purchased enough black fringe to cover ten pillows.

2. Cut the fringe to the size of pillows.

3. Glued the fringe to pillows.

I spent around $250 to complete this project. But I saved $600-$1,200 by not having to buy or recover my existing pillows.

Renew Artwork By Changing The Frame

You don't have to spend a fortune when buying artwork for your home. Savvy shoppers can find great buys at upscale discount stores, estate sales, auctions, garage sales and antique shops.

Another idea is to revamp pieces that you already own by changing the frames or swapping your prints with family members or friends.

When I was searching for two large paintings for my living room, I was thrilled when I happened upon the most beautiful Mediterranean landscape paintings at an upscale discount store.

However, the frames were gold and ornate and they just didn't fit my decorating plan. When I took the pictures home and hung them on the wall they stood out like a sore thumb.

When my husband and kids saw them they were not impressed and I believe the word they used was "gaudy."

I agreed that the frames were gaudy and gold, but I knew I had found an excellent deal. Each canvas was priced at around $1,400, but they were discounted to 70 percent or more. I paid $600 for both. The actual frames were 7 inches wide and they measured 58 by 47 inches. I had priced large frames in the past and they were running around $800 and up.

I knew that I had to change the frames so I called my neighbor, who is an artist, and spoke with her about the project. She suggested that I paint the color of the frames by doing a reverse-antiquing technique.

She helped and we accomplished this by brushing black acrylic paint onto the frames and then wiping it off. In about 4 to 5 hours the whole process was complete and the frames were hanging on the wall. After the restoration, the oils fit perfectly into my color scheme.

If you want to change a painting in your home, here's what you need to do:

The following materials were used for the paint technique.

- Three clean paint brushes 1-inch to 3-inch.

- One clean glass plate.

- One cup of water.

- Plenty of clean rags.

- Two bottles of black acrylic paint Delta Ceramcoat-2 fluid ounces each.

- One bottle of satin exterior/interior Delta Ceramcoat-8 fluid ounces each.

Here's what we did:

- We laid the frame on a large folding table with the painting side up.

- We put newspapers on the floor and wiped the frames with a soft clean cloth.

- We poured a little of the paint onto a clean glass plate and dipped the brush into the paint.

- We applied black paint all over the existing gold frame in small sections.

Immediately after we applied the paint application, we wiped it with a clean cloth to expose some of the gold finish. After the paint dried we applied a varnish with a clean, dry brush. It sealed in the color and gave the frame a satin sheen.

Important suggestions:

- Put on as much paint color as you want depending on the intensity of the color you desire.

- Do small sections at a time. If the paint gets too thick, dip the tip of your brush into the cup of water and pat dry.

- Be careful when painting directly around the print. It's best to remove it if possible. We slipped a white poster board in between the frame and the painting to protect the canvas.

So the next time you see the perfect picture or artwork for your home, but the frame isn't right, take it home and paint it.

Foster Children Need A Space Of Their Own

Q: I am a grandmother raising two foster children. My lifelong goal has always been to help children in need and this is something that I am enjoying very much. I am raising a 10-year-old and a 6-year-old, both girls.

God has blessed me with a spacious home and I am happy to share it with them.

My question is: How can I help these two little girls make the transition to rooming together more bearable and give the littlest one some security and comfort in her new space?

— Genita W.

A: What a blessing you are to all of the children out there without a home. You are truly an inspiration to me and others. It's not easy to open up your home and take on the extra responsibility of raising two young children, at any age.

When you are planning your design make sure that both children have a place in the room that they can call their own. You can divide the closets and put their names above each side on the door. If you need additional storage utilize the space underneath the bed. It's a great spot to place toys and books.

Take a shopping trip and encourage the girls to become involved in the selection of their bedding and other items that are needed for their new space. Encourage them to express their own identities. Maybe you can paint each side of the room a different color.

For a special treat have their names monogrammed on a set of towels and look for throw pillows with inspirational quotes on them. All of these little touches will help them to adjust to their new surroundings and learn to respect each other's things.

Once they have decorated their new room they will want to keep it clean and will take pride in being part of this new family unit.

These Built-ins Are Bumming Me Out!

Q: I need help! I have an older home with a large master bedroom. Everything is built-in, from the vanity to the dresser and even the bed. I can't move anything and it makes me feel closed in. I had a little sofa in here and I took it out and I had a bookcase for a television stand and I switched that out with my exercise equipment.

I am tired of everything. All of the wood is painted in an antique white with a little light blue in it. I recently painted the walls white and replaced the carpet. The window valances and the carpet are a soft blue as well.

What can I do?

— Lula W.

A: One option would be to tear out all of or some of the built-ins and replace them with pieces of furniture that could be easily moved around. This would be a huge undertaking and would probably require the expertise of a carpenter. If you decide on that option, be sure to solicit a few bids prior to selecting a contractor.

The second option is to remove the built-in bed. From your description, this structure is absorbing all of the life out of the room. Once you remove the bed it will open up both the wall space and the ceiling and it will ultimately allow more natural and artificial light to flow into the room, thus giving the space a larger and more open feel.

Your third option is to lighten up the space with paint and furniture selections.

By painting all of the wood work a crisp linen-white and replacing some of the all-wood pieces with wicker, you can achieve a much lighter feel in the room.

The Cottage or Nantucket style would work well in this space.

Incorporate a few pieces of wicker furniture and a pair of free flowing drapes. This will soften the room and diminish some of the hard edges.

Nantucket Gardens and Houses (published by Little, Brown) is a good reference book for this style. The author is Virginia Scott Heard with photography by Taylor Lewis. This book should inspire you and give you tips on real Nantucket-styled homes and good examples of how too accessorize with things you already own.

To complete your dream bedroom concentrate on the *focal point* of the room; which is the bed.

Cover your mattress with down padding for extra comfort and pile on the linens in lots of luxurious layers and pastel colors.

For the finishing touch, add a few throw pillows to your bed with a lemon-drop hue.

Remember, your bedroom is your *comfort zone* and it needs to make you feel at ease the moment you enter your domain. This is one of the most important niches in your home.

If you can't find relaxation in this area, you might end up watching *HGTV* all night.

What's The Skinny On Fringe?

Q: What is the definition of fringe and what can I do with it?

— Karen W.

A: Fringe is a an ornamental border consisting of short straight or twisted threads or strips hanging from cut or raveled edges or from a separate band, according to Webster's New Collegiate dictionary. Fringe can be applied to pillows, drapes, throws, bedspreads and other accessory items. It's also commonly used to trim lamps.

The price range of fringe varies between $1.25 per yard to $50 and up per yard. The price depends on the name brand and the content of the fabric. For example chenille blends are usually more expensive than rayon, polyester or cotton blends.

The size and length of the fringe is also a price factor. Usually the longer the fringe the more it costs.

Two of the most popular brands are *Conso* and *Bomar* and they can be purchased at most fabric stores.

When Is The Right Time To Reupholster My Furniture?

Are you caught in a furniture dilemma?

Should I reupholster my current furniture or should I purchase new pieces?

Do you want a new and fresh look but you don't want to spend a fortune on an entire room of furniture?

Here are a few things to consider:

1. Do you like your existing furniture?

2. Is it top quality and worth reupholstering?

3. Ask yourself: Can I buy similar pieces with the same or better construction and fabric quality for less?

If you can buy a similar piece of furniture for less than you could reupholster an existing one, then you might want to consider buying a new piece.

I have this thing for buying old furniture and having it reupholstered. In my opinion the quality and construction of some of the older pieces are better made than some of the current designs.

Granted, if you spend the money for a designer piece you will usually get the quality, construction and the fabric selections that you desire for a much higher price.

However, if you like the look of older pieces you can find them at garage sales, estate sales and auctions for a great price.

A couple of years ago I purchased a chair for $14 at a second-hand store and had it reupholstered in a leopard print. I also found a wonderful wing-backed chair from the 1940s with a heavy duty frame at a garage sale for $25. The chair now sits in a corner of my bedroom covered in a wine ultra-suede.

One of my favorite finds was a set of *Henredon* stools that I snatched up at a going-out-of-business sale. I covered the stools with a whimsical monkey pattern. To tone down the crackled gold finish I washed the legs with black acrylic paint.

When selecting a company to reupholster your furniture, get references and use a qualified professional.

Hire someone who can rebuild and re-stuff your furniture, not just cover and staple, unless it's something that you want to do yourself.

The price of an upholstered piece depends on the size and the time involved. To recover a standard straight-back chair can range between $150-$300 and up per chair, plus fabric.

A Dining Room Makeover Made Simple

Q: What can I do to add color and drama to my dining room for under $500?

— Saundra B.

A: One of the first things you should do when trying to give your room a little makeover is reposition things to open up the space. Next, add color through your accessories. Make an effort to utilize what you already have in a different or unique way.

Saundra and her husband, Conrad, were exited about my suggestions, so they hired me to help them pull it all together.

Here's what we did:

- To give the room a fresh open feel we placed the dining room table at an angle.

- We went shopping for a couple of pictures to add a punch of color to the walls.

- We placed a large plant in an empty corner of the room to add height and fill up the space.

- They had recently purchased two large floral arrangements. We placed one on top of the china cabinet to draw the eye up and add color and texture to the room.

- We rearranged the china cabinet and pulled out items that were in storage and used them in the space.

- We purchased a table runner that had lots of texture and color.

- We found unused crystal candle holders with tall candles to soften the look of the table.

- We purchased 6 gold shades to spice up her chandelier and we used her silk flowers to add color to the fixture by wrapping it around the chandelier.

- We brought in items from other rooms to achieve a totally new look for their dining room.

During this 6-hour marathon shopping spree, we located all of the necessary accessories to get what they wanted for their comfort zone. And by utilizing items that they already had, they saved a huge amount of money.

Here are some tips to help you change your dining space without breaking the bank:

1. Freshen up the space with paint. It's inexpensive and it can really change the look and feel of a room.

2. Purchase a couple of yards of fabric from the sale bin at a fabric store and drape it over your windows with a simple rod.

3. Buy an additional piece of fabric and bunch it up and place it on your table for a make-shift table runner.

4. Pull out your candlesticks and use different-sized candles to add a dramatic look to your table top.

5. Drape a small table runner or piece of fabric over a picture frame in your china cabinet.

6. Add whimsy by placing an old purse or hat in your china cabinet.

7. Merge crystal or glass with metals like silver or pewter. They reflect off one another and look great under the lights of the table or in the china cabinet.

8. Layer the table with color. Use tablecloths, place mats, and napkins.

9. For unexpected napkin holders, buy individual flowers and keep them in the little water containers that you get at the florist. Take ribbon and tie it around the napkin and then slip the flower underneath the ribbon. (Save the little plastic containers and use them throughout the year. If you don't have any, the florist will sell them to you inexpensively).

Now go out and create your own unique comfort zone!

5

Furniture Resource Guide

Mi-Ling's Favorite Web Sites

Ashley Furniture	www.ashleyfurniture.com
Baker Furniture	www.baker.com
Barcalounger	www.barcalounger.com
Bassett Furniture	www.bassettfurniture.com
Bernhardt Furniture	www.bernhardtfurniture.com
Braxton Culler, Inc.	www.braxtonculler.com
Broyhill Furniture	www.broyhill.com
Casa Stradvari	www.casastradvari.com
Century Furniture	www.centuryfurniture.com
Charleston Forge	www.charlestonforge.com
Classic Gallery	www.classicgallery.com
Clayton Marcus	www.claytonmarcus.com
Comfort Zone Column	www.comfortzonecolumn.com
Douglas Furniture	www.douglasfurniture.com
Drexel Heritage	www.DrexelHeritage.com
Ethan Allen	www.ethanallen.com
Fabrics Unlimited	www.fabricsunlimited.com
Fairfield Chair	www.fairfieldchair.com
Flexsteel Industries, Inc.	www.flexsteel.com
Furniture Brands International	www.furniturebrands.com
Hammary Furniture Company	www.hammary.com
Harden Furniture	www.harden.com
Hekman	www.hekman.com
Henredon	www.Henredon.com
Hickory Chair Company	www.hickorychair.com
Highland House	www.highlandhousefurniture.com
Homecrest Industries	www.homecrest.com
Home Depot	www.homedepot.com
Holland House Furniture	www.hollandhousefurniture.com
Hooker Furniture	www.hookerfurniture.com
Howard Miller	www.howardmiller.com

Huntington House Inc.	www.huntingtonhouse.com
Johnston Casuals Furniture	www.johnstoncasuals.com
Kincaid Furniture	www.kincaidfurniture.com
Klaussner Furniture	www.klaussner.com
L. & J.G. Stickley, Inc.	www.stickley.com
La-Z-Boy, Inc.	www.lazboy.com
The Lane Company	www.lanefurniture.com
Lexington Home Brand	www.Lexington.com
Lloyd/Flanders Industries	www.lloydflanders.com
Lowes	www.lowes.com
Center Maitland-Smith	www.maitland-smith.com
Ask Mi-Ling	www.Mi-Ling.com
Natuzzi	www.Natuzzi.com
Norwalk Furniture Corporation	www.norwalkfurniture.com
O.W. Lee Co.	www.owlee.com
Pearson Company	www.pearsoncompany.com
Pennsylvania House	www.pennsylvaniahouse.com
Pulaski Furniture Company	www.pulaskifurniture.com
Riverside Furniture	www.riversidefurniture.com
Sligh	www.sligh.com
Southwood Furniture Corp.	www.southwoodfurn.com
Stanley Furniture Company	www.stanleyfurniture.com
Telescope Casual	www.telescopecasual.com
Thomasville Furniture	www.thomasville.com
Woodard, Inc.	www.woodard-furniture.com

For more information on decorating go to www.mi-ling.com

About The Author

Mi-Ling Stone Poole grew up in the Twin Cities with some of the major players who developed the *Minneapolis Sound*. These friendships inspired her to pursue a career in the entertainment industry.

After graduating from the University of Kansas with a bachelor's degree in journalism, Mi-Ling worked as a freelance writer, advertising and public relations executive and a radio and television host.

In 1991, she decided to form Exact Image Entertainment Group and focused on booking and promoting celebrity speakers and entertainers. Her first celebrity client was actor Esther Rolle, best known for her portrayal of Florida Evans, on the hit television show *Good Times*.

One of the highlights of her career was working as associate producer on "Ninth Street," an independent film featuring Martin Sheen and Isaac Hayes, which later won an Independent Film Channel Award.

After a successful career in the entertainment industry, Mi-Ling went back to school and earned her master's degree in communications from Oklahoma City University.

In 2001, she decided to merge her love for journalism with her passion for decorating and began writing two weekly decorating columns; *Ask Mi-Ling,* and *Mi-Ling's Comfort Zone*. These columns are published weekly in newspapers throughout the country and have been translated and published in Spanish. Currently, she writes a weekly decorating column for *The Oklahoman* in Oklahoma City.

Mi-Ling earned the reputation of being funny, entertaining and outspoken during her weekly radio segments, while offering advice and cost-saving tips on decorating. She believes that creating a comfortable and livable home is the key to a great design.

www.mi-ling.com

Decorating Notes

978-0-595-38310-8
0-595-38310-6

Printed in the United States
50691LVS00003B/220-243